SpringerBriefs in Business

SpringerBriefs in Organisational Studies

Series Editor
Jan Jonker, Radbound University Nijmegen, Nijmegen, The Netherlands

The concept of the industrial organisation is rapidly changing. So does the landscape of what we can and must organise. As a consequence the role and function of organisation in society is subject of a vivid debate. New needs and demands of stakeholders, (governance) scandals and growing depletion of resources all put pressure on established practices. This series addresses a wide variety of the problems and issues related to the contemporary business enterprise. Possible themes could be stakeholder management, risk, sustainable development, recycling and waste, corporate responsibility, multiple value creation, strategic alliances, innovation and change and transition. Manuscripts can address those problems and issues related specifically to a sector–yet this is not mandatory. The ambition is to build over time a series that serves as a landmark.

Ian I. Mitroff

The Socially Responsible Organization

Lessons from COVID

Ian I. Mitroff
Mitroff Crisis Management
Berkeley, CA, USA

This book is an open access publication.

ISSN 2191-5482　　　　　　　ISSN 2191-5490　(electronic)
SpringerBriefs in Business

ISSN 2570-3439　　　　　　　ISSN 2570-3447　(electronic)
SpringerBriefs in Organisational Studies

ISBN 978-3-030-99807-3　　　ISBN 978-3-030-99808-0　(eBook)
https://doi.org/10.1007/978-3-030-99808-0

© The Author(s) 2022
Open Access This book is licensed under the terms of the Creative Commons Attribution 4.0 International License (http://creativecommons.org/licenses/by/4.0/), which permits use, sharing, adaptation, distribution and reproduction in any medium or format, as long as you give appropriate credit to the original author(s) and the source, provide a link to the Creative Commons license and indicate if changes were made.
The images or other third party material in this book are included in the book's Creative Commons license, unless indicated otherwise in a credit line to the material. If material is not included in the book's Creative Commons license and your intended use is not permitted by statutory regulation or exceeds the permitted use, you will need to obtain permission directly from the copyright holder.
The use of general descriptive names, registered names, trademarks, service marks, etc. in this publication does not imply, even in the absence of a specific statement, that such names are exempt from the relevant protective laws and regulations and therefore free for general use.
The publisher, the authors and the editors are safe to assume that the advice and information in this book are believed to be true and accurate at the date of publication. Neither the publisher nor the authors or the editors give a warranty, expressed or implied, with respect to the material contained herein or for any errors or omissions that may have been made. The publisher remains neutral with regard to jurisdictional claims in published maps and institutional affiliations.

This Springer imprint is published by the registered company Springer Nature Switzerland AG
The registered company address is: Gewerbestrasse 11, 6330 Cham, Switzerland

This book is dedicated to my grandson, Jonah Benjamin Silvers, in the firm knowledge that he will help create a better world.

Contents

1. **The Assault on Reason: The Major Arguments in Defense of Not Getting Vaccinated for Covid 19** 1
   The Principal Arguments/Claims 2
   Postscript. 6
   Reflections. 6
2. **The Assault on Reason, Part Two: A Deeper Analysis**. 9
   Reflections. 13
3. **Infrastructure Wars: The Politization of Everything** 15
   Four Perspectives 16
   The Toulmin Argumentation Framework (TAF). 18
   Reflections. 19
4. **Regulating Tech Is Only Half of the Job**. 21
   Reflections. 23
5. **The Socially Responsible Organization: The Critical Cast of Players** . . 25
   Postscript: Meta Mistakes: It's All in a Name 28
   Reflections. 29
6. **Dis Versus Mis-Information: Unexpected Insights from Covid19** 31
   Postscript: A Needed Success Story 33
   Reflections. 34
7. **Compromise Is Key to Our Learning to Live Together: The Resolution of Key Issues Is Not Possible Without It** 35
   Reflections. 36
8. **Coping with a Complex Messy World: Education for the Twenty-First Century and Beyond** 39

Epilogue 45

Index. 49

Foreword

This book owes its origin to the continuous outpouring of false, disingenuous, and downright dangerous arguments/claims that have constantly been bandied about in favor of <u>*NOT*</u> getting vaccinated for Covid-19. They are nothing less than the most despicable attempts to justify harmful and utterly irresponsible behavior. Not only do they represent serious threats to our collective health and well-being but they also constitute major threats to our collective reason and sanity as well.

In short, the outright refusal to accept the reality of Covid-19 is the clearest indication that we are suffering from Mass Psychosis.

The arguments are bad enough by themselves, but the emotions behind them are even worse. They're so deeply laden with hate that they've led to explicit death threats towards those Public Health Officials who've dared mandate the wearing of masks to help control the Virus.[1] Combatting them is thereby one of the central aims of the book.

Given that Social Media, most notably Facebook, have played a key role in the dissemination of fallacious arguments and information about the vaccines, hi-tech organizations are a major part of the problem as well. They're certainly a major factor in the decline in Civic Responsibly. As such, they're an integral part of the Pandemic. It's especially onerous since it was not anticipated, taken into account, and therefore planned for.

Some of the most atrocious examples of irresponsibility are found in the arguments that the Tech giants use to justify their egregious behavior. That Facebook deliberately pursued policies that it knew caused serious harm to young girls is not only completely reprehensible but also unconscionable. It's one of the worst examples of putting profits, no matter how they're obtained, ahead of the well-being of its most vulnerable users. As a result, there is no worse example of the Socially Irresponsible Organization. For this reason alone, elucidating the nature of The Socially Responsible Organization and the larger responsibilities we share as Global

---

[1] Mike Baker and Danielle Ivory, "Public Health Crisis Grows With Distrust and Threats," <u>The New York Times,</u> Monday, October 18, 2021, pp. A1 and A14.

Citizens is thereby one of the chief topics of the book. It's certainly one of its main thrusts.

In talking about The Socially Responsible Organization, we are thereby talking about The Socially Responsible Society as well. Indeed, the two are deeply intertwined, if not inseparable. It's impossible to have one without the other.

In combatting the multitude of threats we face, Crisis Management plays a central role. Undeniably, it's one of the key pillars of The Socially Responsible Organization. We have every right to insist that before any organization is allowed to operate, they need to demonstrate on an on-going basis that they have done everything in their power to anticipate the worst that can happen as a result of the unintended consequences, including the abuses and misuses of their products and services. Even more, they are obligated to do everything they can to thwart it. In short, the potential for crises is so great that we have every right to mandate Crisis Management as a prime requirement for being allowed to operate.

In sum, the book is about surfacing some of the most critical arguments on which our lives depend and then subjecting them to the strongest possible scrutiny and critique we can muster. They deserve nothing less. Critical Thinking has never been more essential.

Nonetheless, I would be remiss if I failed to note that sadly many of those who are under the grip of the arguments/claims for not getting vaccinated are so completely under their power that virtually nothing will convince them to give them up. As true as this is, it only reinforces even more the need to do everything we can to arm those who think otherwise with the best counterarguments possible so that they can stand up to them as much as possible.

In the broadest sense, it's about the skills necessary to cope with a complex, messy world.

Professor Emeritus,
USC Senior Research Affiliate,
Center for Catastrophic Risk Management,
UC Berkeley.

Ian I. Mitroff

Acknowledgement

Selected portions have previously appeared in blogs in <u>The Nation of Change</u>.

> The polarization of American society has become a national security threat, acting as a barrier for combatting catastrophes and thwarting external dangers. Partisan spectacles during the global covid-19 pandemic have undermined the country's international standing as a model of liberal democracy and eroded its authority on public health...[1]

---

[1] Fiona Hill, "The Kremlin's Strange Victory," <u>Foreign Affairs</u>, November/December 2021, p. 46.

Chapter 1
The Assault on Reason: The Major Arguments in Defense of Not Getting Vaccinated for Covid 19

> …the savage and changeable winds of public opinion demanded ever more paranoid and grandiose statements. U.S. plans for state building and counterinsurgency became issues of evasion and euphemism, justified with contorted logic, dressed in partial statistics, and decorated with false analogies. They were inflexible, simplistic, and shrilly confident…[1]

> The results of a new poll shared exclusively with Yahoo News finds that 28 percent of U.S. adults believe without evidence that the 'truth about the harmful effects of vaccines' is being deliberately hidden from the public.[2]

"From which top-ranked Medical School did you graduate at the top of your class such that you're a world-renowned expert in contagious diseases?" is the proper response to such outrageous claims.

Most of all, the chapter offers an incisive critique of the arguments. While counterarguments are generally ineffective in convincing their staunchest proponents to abandon their positions in the light of disconfirming evidence and information, they play an indispensable role in providing needed support for those who are in doubt and open to reason. Whether they persuade their proponents or not, they are absolutely necessary in preserving our basic sense of sanity.

One of the most significant outcomes of the chapter is the finding that the individual arguments readily group into distinct clusters thus bolstering one another in even more insidious ways. For instance, the Hoax and Invulnerability Clusters are two of the more prominent. In the first, the Virus is a complete Hoax that does not deserve to be taken seriously. In the second, even if it is, I'm Invulnerable to it. But surely the most important of all is the Freedom Cluster, namely that it's my fundamental right to determine what's done to me and my body.

---

[1] Rory Stewart, "The Last Days of Insurrection," <u>Foreign Affairs</u>, November/December 2021, p.66.
[2] Caitlin Dickson, Yahoo News, Tuesday, November 23, 2021.

© The Author(s) 2022
I. I. Mitroff, *The Socially Responsible Organization*, SpringerBriefs in Business, https://doi.org/10.1007/978-3-030-99808-0_1

Just as important is the realization that the same clusters apply to virtually all of the Hot Button Issues with which we're faced. In this way, they play a larger role by helping to illuminate the true sources of the general difficulties facing us.

The Principal Arguments/Claims

Given that our lives literally rest on the soundness of the "arguments"—if they're even worthy of the term--that have been constantly bandied about in favor of *NOT* getting vaccinated for Covid19, they deserve the most intense scrutiny and critique we can muster. Each is bad enough in and of itself, but taken together, they reinforce one another by all-too-easily bunching together in distinct clusters thereby reinforcing one another in the most insidious of ways.

But by far, one of their worst features is the sheer anger, fury, and outright hate that underscores them. Threats of harm and violence towards those who don't share the same views as their proponents are too close for comfort. Indeed, those Public Health Officials who've taken their responsibilities seriously and thus have mandated the wearing of masks to protect against the spread of the Virus have been subject to explicit death threats.[3]

It's made worse by the constant threats of violence that are a part of U.S. Society. Thus, a frontpage article in The New York Times reported that at a Conservative rally in Western Idaho, a young man stepped up to a microphone and asked, "when he could start killing Democrats."[4] Harboring such thoughts in private is bad enough, but expressing them openly is crossing a dangerous line. The all-too-real fear is that it will lead to actual violence. Sadly, the same kinds of intense emotions underlie each of the arguments/claims.

Although we will encounter more as we proceed, the following are representative of the kinds of arguments/claims that have been advanced in favor of *NOT* getting vaccinated. They are nothing less than the most reprehensible justifications for utterly appalling and irresponsible behavior of the worst kind:

1. "By virtue of my age, health, lifestyle, and special circumstances, I'm totally immune to the Virus."
2. "My body, my choice! The Government has no right to tell me what I can and cannot do with my body. It's an infringement on my Basic Freedoms and Liberties! It's nothing less than Tyranny. Besides, I and I alone know best when it comes to my own body."

---

[3] Baker and Ivory, Op cit.
[4] Lisa Lerer and Amstead W. Herndon, "Menace Grows Commonplace G.O.P.: Threats Are Embraced as Divide Widens," The New York Times, Saturday, November 13, 2021, p. A1.
Billy Perrigo/Paris, "Change Agent," Time, December 6/13, 2021, p. 43.

3. "The Bible tells us that we are made in the Direct Image of God. Wearing masks is nothing less than a Grievous Defilement of His Image. It's a Sin of the Gravest Order!"
4. "The vaccines are responsible for causing the Virus."
5. "The authorities have reversed themselves so many times such that they're not to be trusted."
6. "The Virus is not a big deal."
7. "The wearing of masks is foolish."
8. "We cannot allow science and scientists to rule our lives. Who gave Anthony Fauci the power to make decisions over us?"
9. "It's time to stop worrying about others."
10. "The Virus is part of Nature. Thus, in harmony with all things, it's morally and universally appropriate to let Nature run its course."
11. "The vaccines are an insidious plot by the Government to put microchips in us not just to track our every whereabouts, but even worse, to read and thereby control our minds."

The first claim is that by virtue of a person's special circumstances, and/or basic characteristics, he, she, or they are totally exempt from the disease, thus requiring no intervention or treatment whatsoever. The rebuttal is that there are no such known characteristics or circumstances that make anyone immune. To believe otherwise is wishful thinking of the most fanciful kind. It's made even worse by the fact that it's a direct threat to the health and well-being of others. In this sense, it's not merely "wishful," but absolutely "dangerous."

The second is a complete misunderstanding of the concept of Freedom. Freedom does not mean that one has the absolute or sole right to do whatever he, she, or they pleases. By definition, all civilized societies put strict limits and clear restraints on what their citizens can and cannot do. They are absolutely necessary to protect the general health, safety, and well-being of society as a whole. The acceptance of limits is in fact one of the key things that binds a diverse set of people together into a collective body of One.

In curbing the spread of deadly diseases, Public Health Mandates are clearly within the proper scope of Government. To believe otherwise only reinforces the serious need for greater Civics Education.

Even more basic, one is not always the best judge when it comes to one's body. It's impossible for anyone to possess all of the relevant knowledge that experts have acquired though years of arduous and specialized training.

The outstanding case where "my body my choice" does apply is a woman's basic right to choose whether to have an abortion or not. Indeed, having an abortion is not a communicable disease like the Virus. You don't "catch it from others." In this sense, a woman's right to choose constitutes a Closed System whereas the decision to get a vaccine or not constitutes an Open System in that it affects the health and well-being of countless others.

Of course, Right-to-Lifers feel the exact opposite. For them, the attitude that having an abortion is morally acceptable is directly akin to a communicable disease.

Unfortunately, the right to have an abortion is facing its most serious challenges in decades.

The third is a gross misreading and interpretation of the Bible, or any particular text for that matter. The inherent nature, let alone the image, of God is not defiled by the wearing of protective equipment, especially that which safeguards the health and well-being of our fellow citizens. To the contrary, it's testimony to our God-given intelligence and the ability to exercise it wisely.

The claim that the vaccines are responsible for the Virus is not only completely bogus, but a total misunderstanding and complete reversal of the correct order of things. The "correct sequence" is that the Virus is responsible for the rapid, but safe development of the vaccines and the protection they clearly offer from the disease, not the reverse. It's part of the false belief that the Government deliberately planted the Virus in the vaccines in order to make us sick and thereby control us. It's reflective of the low trust in institutions of all kinds, a condition that has been worsening for decades.

It's true that authorities such as CDC and Dr. Fauci have reversed themselves. But they have not done so arbitrarily. Rather, they have changed their recommendations as the underlying conditions themselves have changed. Indeed, one of the prime features of Science is that it's self-correcting. As a matter of fact, it generally goes out of its way to reward those who disprove earlier notions. Ideally, the institutions that are based on it are self-correcting as well.

This is not to say that the CDC has always been in tight alignment with other agencies such as the FDA. In something as complex as Covid 19, it would be an absolute miracle if all of them were in perfect agreement all of the time.

The Virus is a big deal, Period! It's one of the worst calamities to strike in modern times. It's responsible for over 5 million deaths and its continually getting worse. Further, new more dangerous variants are constantly emerging.

Furthermore, in response to another variation on the same theme, it's not a hoax created by Nefarious Liberals to impose their will on others, certainly not to eliminate and thereby replace Conservatives.

To the contrary, not wearing masks is foolish. Along with being vaccinated, masks are one of the best protections we have. Recent studies only confirm it.

Dr. Fauci earned his position by virtue of his specialized education, years of experience, and outstanding qualifications. No one "gave it to him."

When indeed is it ever time to stop being concerned about others? Aren't we all in this together? Do we really want no one to be concerned about anyone other than him, herself, or they? If so, it would be the absolute end to society as we know it. Indeed, it would lead us backwards before the advent of modern civilized societies where everyone was completely out for themselves and no one else.

The Virus is not the result of "Nature acting alone" for there is no such thing anymore. It's the result of humans not taking appropriate precautions to prevent animals from all-too-easily transmitting a deadly disease from one species to another. In today's world, there's little humans do that does not affect all of Nature. The most potent example is the 2020 Nobel prize in Chemistry that was awarded for gene-editing technology. While it was created for the express purpose of correcting genetic effects in young babies, the fear is that in the wrong hands it can and will be used to create "designer humans." Once again, there's not a single aspect of Nature that is not affected by our actions, intended or not.

The last would be laughable if it were not conspiratorial thinking of the worst kind.

Once again, the individual arguments/claims are bad enough in and of themselves, but they're made even worse by the fact that they all-too-readily group together in distinct clusters thereby reinforcing one another even more.

First and foremost is the Hoax Cluster, namely that Virus is not real, and as a result, not deserving of any serious attention. It's supported by the false contention that the numbers of people affected are too small for us to worry about. It's reinforced by the Conspiracy/Paranoia Cluster. Namely, the Virus has been deliberately fomented by the Government so that not only can it track our whereabouts and thoughts at all times, but control them and thereby take away our God-given Freedoms and Rights. The I Know Best Cluster is more of the same. Another is the Invulnerability Cluster, namely that "If in the highly improbable case that the Virus is real, I'm immune to it." The Product Defect Cluster is the unfounded claim that the Vaccines, not the Virus, are the true danger since they're responsible for causing the Virus in the first place. In addition, the Vaccines have not been tested enough to ensure their absolute safety.

Arguably, the notion of Freedom is deserving of a distinct cluster of its own. For in many ways, the notion of Freedom is the prime animating force behind each of the arguments/claims. In short, "No one has the right to tell me what I can and cannot do with my body."

In the same vein, the Distrust of those in Authority also ranks high.

While the preceding do not cover them all, they capture the general spirit of the major arguments/claims that have been put forth. Indeed, new ones are constantly emerging.

One of the worst was in the form of a protest outside the office of New York State Assemblyman, Jeffrey Dinowitz who is Jewish. Demonstrators wore Nazi symbols to express their opposition to the vaccines. To equate in any way the taking of vaccines with the Holocaust is nothing less than Contemptible and Evil!

In the end, all of the above and more are symptomatic of the general failure to inculcate Critical Thinking and Civic Responsibility in society at large. Their failure is especially pernicious for Critical Thinking and Civic Responsibility are the very foundations of democratic societies. They cannot exist without them. Without the ability to reason critically from premises which have themselves been subject to serious examination, Reason itself cannot be trusted. And without Reason how can anything be established, let alone trusted?

It cannot be said enough. Without an understanding and acceptance of Civic Responsibility, society is not possible.

Nonetheless, as we show in the next chapter, the situation is even worse. It's symptomatic of widespread Mental Disorders.

Finally, there is another aspect which deserves special mention. Efforts are of course underway to learn the lessons of Covid19 so that we're better prepared for the next Pandemics. Indeed, Epidemiologists have been warning for years that it was only a matter of "when" not "if" that a major Pandemic would strike. To better our understanding and thereby encourage our preparations, they've even conducted simulations for future Pandemics. But no one to my knowledge has proposed, let alone performed, actual simulations of all the systems that would be affected by a major Pandemic: the Economy, Hospitals, Nursing Homes, Schools, etc. It's the result of our failure to think and act Systemically. In fact, who anticipated the awful arguments/claims that would result in response to the Pandemic?

The situation is made worse by the fact that the situation is not entirely without precedent. There have always been fallacious and demented arguments in response to previous horrific outbreaks such as HIV and SARS. But why didn't we learn from them and thus be better prepared? If we had, would it have upped the rates of vaccinations? Would it have helped stemmed the spread of the Virus?

If we are to do better, it will not only require the cooperation of diverse experts to plan for the serious Medical, Economic, and Social consequences of the next Pandemics, but it will require Experts of diverse stripes to anticipate as many of the outlandish and outright bizarre arguments/claims that that will surely follow. Such planning can no longer be left to chance. Even if it only helps to persuade a few, the effort is worth it.

Thinking and Preparing for the Unthinkable has never been more critical.

Postscript

The hasty actions by over 20 states to pass laws prohibiting the teaching of Critical Race Theory—more broadly, anything that makes students feel uncomfortable—shows the power of the Invulnerability Cluster. Only in this case, it's twisted around such that the emphasis is on Vulnerability. The fear is that by teaching the true history of race relations in the U.S., students will not only be indoctrinated, but White students in particular will be made to feel bad about themselves. In this way, Paranoia plays a central role as well[5].

Reflections

As you read the various arguments and counterarguments, what were your personal feelings? Did they affect you in any way? Do you personally know anyone who has espoused any of them? Have they led you to feel estranged from any members of your family or close friends? Do the counterarguments help you in any way in combatting the main arguments/claims?

---

[5] Patricia J. Williams, "How Not to Talk About RACE," The Nation, November 1/8. 2021, pp. 14–17, 23.

Open Access This chapter is licensed under the terms of the Creative Commons Attribution 4.0 International License (http://creativecommons.org/licenses/by/4.0/), which permits use, sharing, adaptation, distribution and reproduction in any medium or format, as long as you give appropriate credit to the original author(s) and the source, provide a link to the Creative Commons license and indicate if changes were made.

The images or other third party material in this chapter are included in the chapter's Creative Commons license, unless indicated otherwise in a credit line to the material. If material is not included in the chapter's Creative Commons license and your intended use is not permitted by statutory regulation or exceeds the permitted use, you will need to obtain permission directly from the copyright holder.

Chapter 2
The Assault on Reason, Part Two: A Deeper Analysis

If these weren't bad enough, we're dealing with Demented Thinking on nothing less than on a collective basis. Thus, Conservative Talk-Radio Host Dennis Prager declared that he deliberately caught Covid 19 because he believes that Natural Immunity is better than that which is conferred by the vaccines. Crazy Making is thereby the major order of the day!

The point is that combatting such arguments is not merely a case of correcting faulty Logic and thinking, but of dealing with Widespread Mental Disturbance. Indeed, they constitute threats of the highest order to the Collective Mental Health of the nation and the world as a whole.

Given that those who are most in need of Psychotherapy are often the most reluctant to get it, and even if they weren't, there're not enough qualified Psychotherapists to go around, what then can we do? Among the only remaining alternatives is Healthy Leadership at the highest levels to address our deepest fears and do everything they can to calm and reassure us.

But worst of all, we have to confront the fact that some people are so damaged by whatever traumas they've experienced in the past such that they are unable to trust anyone, let alone authority figures urging them to get vaccinated. They've been betrayed so often and so deeply such that they are impervious to rational appeals. Never again will they allow themselves to be misled by anyone.

Chapter 1 presented an analysis of the validity of the "arguments"—if they are even deserving of the term—that have been bandied about in favor of *NOT* getting vaccinated for Covid 19. In a word, it exposed the serious defects in reasoning behind each of the major arguments/claims. Unfortunately, as necessary as this is, it doesn't get to the real roots of the problem, the underlying states of mind that are responsible for them in the first place. A deeper, Psychological analysis is called for if we are to understand why they arise in the first place, and secondly, exert such a hold on their proponents.

However, while absolutely necessary, such an analysis is not without its own problems. Many find it extremely disturbing to leave the reassuring realms of Logic and Reason where supposedly matters are subject to clear-cut rules and procedures, and thus can be determined and settled with complete confidence. To enter into the realm of Psychology often raises as much anxiety as the original issues themselves. Nonetheless, as distressing as it is—indeed, precisely because it is—it's all the more necessary.

To reiterate, the following are the major arguments/claims for not getting vaccinated. Indeed, they cannot be emphasized enough:

1. "By virtue of my age, health, lifestyle, and special circumstance, I'm totally immune to the Virus."
2. "My body, my choice! The government has no right to tell me what I can and cannot do with my body. It's an infringement on my Basic Freedoms and Liberties! It's nothing less than Tyranny. Besides, I and I alone know best when it comes to my own body."
3. "The Bible tells us that we are made in the Image of God. Wearing masks is nothing less than a desecration of His Image. It's a Sin of the Gravest Order!"
4. "The vaccine is responsible for causing the Virus."
5. "The authorities have reversed themselves so many times that they're not to be trusted."
6. "The Virus is not a big deal."
7. "The wearing of masks is foolish."
8. "We cannot allow science and scientists to rule our lives. Who gave Anthony Fauci the power to make decisions over us?"
9. "It's time to stop worrying about others."
10. "The Virus is part of Nature. Thus, in harmony with all things, it's morally and universally appropriate to let Nature run its course."
11. "The vaccines are an insidious plot to put microchips in us not just to track our whereabouts, but even worse, to read and thereby control our minds."

To reiterate as well, the first claim is that by virtue of a person's special circumstances, and/or basic characteristics, he, she or they are totally exempt from the disease, therefore requiring no intervention or treatment whatsoever. If ever there were, it's not only a clear-cut, but a classic case of Omnipotent Thinking, if not Grandiosity. It's direct compensation for the fact that the Virus has instilled a deep sense of powerlessness and outright dread in far too many of us. Unfortunately, dismissing the need for protection is not only a direct threat to one's own health and well-being, but to countless others as well.

The second is not only a complete misunderstanding of Freedom, but is a classic example of Narcissism writ large. It cannot be said enough. Freedom does not mean that one has the absolute right to do whatever he, she, or they pleases without any consideration of how others will be affected. Society is not possible without a serious concern for others. The nasty truth is that when one is under the grip of Narcisstic Thinking, only the Self and the Self Alone matters. Indeed, the situation is so awful and terrifying that it borders on Pathological Narcissism.

Even more basic, one is not always the best judge when it comes to one's body. It's impossible for anyone to possess all of the relevant knowledge that experts have acquired though years of arduous and specialized training. To believe otherwise is a further expression of Grandiosity, a highly inflated and thereby unwarranted sense of one's self worth.

Once again, it's also an expression of the deep distrust of and hostility towards authority of any kind.

The third claim suffers similarly in the sense that one is supposedly the best interpreter of the Word of God. Thus, while debasing others in authority, one is a supreme authority onto oneself.

The claim that the vaccine is responsible for the Virus is not only completely bogus, but a total misunderstanding and complete reversal of the correct order of things. The "correct sequence" is that the Virus is responsible for promoting the rapid, but safe, creation of the vaccines and the protection they offer from the disease, not the reverse. To think otherwise is nothing less than a primary case of a major Thought Disorder. In different words, it's a major example of Demented and Delusional Thinking. Given that it flows directly from the false belief that the Government has deliberately placed the Virus in the vaccines in order to destroy White people, it's a clear-cut case of Paranoia as well. It's certainly a reflection of the low trust in Government. Indeed, as such, it's been steadily declining for decades.

The fifth claim is a direct expression of the obsessive need for Certainty. Again, it's true that authorities such as the CDC and Dr. Fauci have reversed themselves. But they have not done so arbitrarily. Rather, they have changed their recommendations as the underlying conditions themselves have changed. Indeed, one of the prime features of Science is that it's generally self-correcting. Again, those who disprove earlier ideas are generally rewarded, although often not without considerable pushback and resistance from their originators and defenders. Unfortunately, change itself is a major threat to far too many.

The Virus is a big deal, Period! It's one of the worst calamities to strike in modern times. It's responsible for over 5 million deaths worldwide and counting. Reducing its magnitude is the only way in which many can cope with a disaster that once again one feels powerless to control. It's as pure a case of Denial and Disavowal as one could ever hope to find.

So is the attitude that wearing masks is foolish.

Demeaning Dr. Fauci is but another form of asserting one's significance, and thereby an inflated sense of one's self-worth and importance. In addition, it cannot be said enough that it's fundamentally a case of the deep distrust of authority of any kind.

Lack of concern about others is another instance of Primary Narcissism. Aren't we all in this together? Do we really want no one to be concerned about anyone other than him, herself, or they? Society itself cannot exist without a basic concern for others.

To reiterate, the Virus is not the result of "Nature acting alone" for there is no such thing anymore. It's the case of humans not taking appropriate precautions to prevent animals from all-too-easily transmitting a deadly disease from one species to another. In today's world, there's little humans do that does not affect all of Nature. To believe otherwise is another case of Denial. It's also a classic case of

Compartmentalization, namely the false belief that causes and effects can be strictly confined and separated so that they do not affect one another, let alone a system as a whole.

The last would be laughable if it were not a clear-cut example of Paranoia.

To reiterate a key point, the individual arguments/claims are bad enough by themselves, but they're made even worse by the fact that they all-too-readily group together in distinct clusters thereby reinforcing one another even more.

First and foremost is the Hoax Cluster, namely that Virus is not real, and as a result, not deserving of any, let alone serious, attention. It's supported by the false assertion that the numbers of people affected are too small for us to worry about. It's reinforced by the Conspiracy/Paranoia Cluster. Namely, the Virus has been fomented by the Government so that not only can it track our whereabouts and thoughts at all times, but control them and thereby take away our God-given freedoms and rights. The I Know Best Cluster is more of the same. Another is the Invulnerability Cluster, namely that "If in the highly improbable case that the Virus is real, I'm immune to it." The Product Defect Cluster is the unfounded claim that the Vaccines, not the Virus, are the true danger since they're responsible for causing the Virus in the first place. In addition, the Vaccines have not been tested sufficiently to ensure their absolute safety.

And as we said earlier, the notion of Freedom is deserving of a Cluster of its own. Indeed, it's one of the primary forces motivating the entire resistance to the taking of the vaccines. But then Freedom is also closely allied with the Distrust of Authorities, which is thereby deserving of its own distinct Cluster as well.

But the absolute worst of all is equating the Holocaust to mandates for the vaccines. How can anyone equate one of the most evil episodes in human history with the taking of vaccines for protection against a deadly disease?

All of the above and more are testimony to the fact that far more than we'd like to believe, we are the prisoners of deep Psychological forces which seriously impede our abilities to reason and think critically. Indeed, just the list itself is overwhelming: Demented and Omnipotent Thinking, Grandiosity, Thought Disorders, Compartmentalization, the Obsessive Need for Certainty, Denial, Disavowal, Paranoia, and Narcissism.

Unfortunately, countering them is not just a matter of accurately identifying the states of mind responsible for each of the so-called arguments/claims. Rather, it's a case of dealing with the pernicious forces that keep us from treating the momentous issues facing us with the clarity of thought and strength of mind they require.

While each of the various arguments/claims are due to over exaggerating fears with regard to forces over which we have little control, it's not an exaggeration to say that as a society we are suffering from serious bouts of Collective Mental Illness, at the very least Serious Mental Distress. Sadly, even if enough were willing to see a Psychotherapist in order to deal with the serious issues from which they are suffering, there are not enough qualified Therapists to fulfill the need.

Who then but our national leaders are available to soothe what ails us? It calls for those who are adept at addressing the unmitigated fears and anxieties we are experiencing without using off-putting labels and talking down to us.

It means frankly acknowledging the Fears that the Virus has unleashed and then providing as realistic an assessment of them as possible. But even more, it means not overwhelming us with mountains of cold-hearted facts, but treating us with empathy. The balance between the two is so important such that we visit the matter repeatedly.

Reflections

As you read an analysis of the arguments from a very different perspective, what were your personal feelings and thoughts? Did they affect you in any way? Does the discussion help you? Do you know anyone personally that is suffering from any one of the maladies described in the chapter? Are they in need of serious help? Has it made it difficult to talk with others who deny their vulnerabilities?

Open Access This chapter is licensed under the terms of the Creative Commons Attribution 4.0 International License (http://creativecommons.org/licenses/by/4.0/), which permits use, sharing, adaptation, distribution and reproduction in any medium or format, as long as you give appropriate credit to the original author(s) and the source, provide a link to the Creative Commons license and indicate if changes were made.

The images or other third party material in this chapter are included in the chapter's Creative Commons license, unless indicated otherwise in a credit line to the material. If material is not included in the chapter's Creative Commons license and your intended use is not permitted by statutory regulation or exceeds the permitted use, you will need to obtain permission directly from the copyright holder.

Chapter 3
Infrastructure Wars: The Politization of Everything

> The natural world obeys no sovereign boundaries, and neither does the worsening ecological crisis…It is time to govern the world as if the earth mattered. What the world needs is a paradigm shift in U.S. foreign policy and international relations—a shift that is rooted in ecological realism and that moves cooperation on shared environmental threats to center stage. Call this new worldview 'planetary politics.'…[1]

It does it by contrasting four very different perspectives: Short-Term Technical, Long-Term Technical, Long-Term People-Oriented, and Short-Term People-Oriented. Not only do they illustrate the intense divides due to sharp differences regarding how different Personality Types approach the issue of Infrastructure, but how it's become deeply politicized as well. As such, it's a stand-in for all other Hot Button Issues facing us.

Importantly, each of the different perspectives has a different take on the Clusters of Chaps. 1 and 2.

Even though none of the four perspectives are able to realize their intended aims without the intense cooperation and support of the others, they are critical in illuminating the great Political Divide that separates us. In short, they are not only illustrative of the Politization of the Mind, but of everything. Bridging them if one can is a challenge of the highest order.

Infrastructure is of course just one of many issues on which we are bitterly divided. In particular, the results help shed additional light on the reactions to the Mandates for the wearing masks.

Most important of all, it shows the critical roles that the different perspectives play in overcoming the arguments/claims with regard to not getting vaccinated.

Even though the House of Representatives has given its go-ahead on the first part of the Infrastructure Bill, it does not take away from the fact that the whole matter is and will likely remain highly politicized, indeed for years to come. In fact, there is no aspect of our existence that is not. The persistent arguments over Infrastructure

---

[1] Stewart M. Patrick, "The International Order Isn't Ready for the Climate Crisis; The Case for a New Planetary Politics, " Foreign Affairs, November/December 2021, p. 166–167.

are a textbook example of the intense divisions that divide us. Not only is Infrastructure a pressing problem in and of itself, but it's a metaphor for what ails us in general.

While the opposing arguments are not necessarily fallacious, at least not in the same ways that those in first two chapters are, they fall seriously short in others that are just as serious. While they typically consider themselves to be superior to and totally independent of their counterparts, none of them can succeed without the intense cooperation and support of the others. They are more dependent on one another than they are both willing and able to admit. But this is only part of the problem.

There is another important reason for examining them. At the end of Chap. 2, we stressed the need to strike a balance between performing "honest, realistic assessments" of the fears associated with Covid 19 versus addressing the deep emotions behind them, namely how much of the Truth people can bear to hear and thus accept. As such, they need to work together, not in opposition. Working towards such a balance is one of the chief aims of the chapter.

Four Perspectives

No matter what the issue, large or small, four very different perspectives are constantly battling for supremacy. With regard to current events, the situation has become so bad that they've hardened into opposing camps. Their followers demand nothing less than complete allegiance to their respective positions. In this sense, they share a great deal in common with the issues of Chaps. 1 and 2.

The first is Short-Term Technical; second, Long-Term Technical; third, Long-Term Human-Centered; and fourth, Short-Term Human-Centered. Those who are familiar with the Myers-Briggs Personality Type Indicator (MBPTI) will immediately recognize these as four of the major Personality Types: Sensing-Thinking or ST for short; Intuitive-Thinking or NT; Intuitive-Feeling or NF; and Sensing-Feeling or SF.

For those whose personalities is governed by a Short-Term Technical or ST perspective, Infrastructure is not just "primarily," but "solely Physical." It consists only of Physical Structures such as Roads, Bridges, and Buildings. Nothing else even comes close, and thus qualifies in any way.

For those whose personalities is governed by a Long-Term Technical or NT perspective, Infrastructure is Systemic. It not only includes Roads, Bridges, and Buildings, but most important of all, it encompasses all of the diverse means by which we connect with one another in a world that is totally interconnected. Broadband is thereby not only an integral, but an essential component in today's world. It's especially concerned with ensuring that new technologies are not only allowed to flourish but are protected from nefarious actors who can bring down the entire System. In this way, Cyber-Security is of paramount importance. It's also deeply concerned with the Physical Health of the planet as a whole. Climate Change is thus a major concern as well.

Four Perspectives   17

In short, whereas ST focuses on details and getting them right, NT focuses on Seeing The Big Picture.

For those whose personalities is governed primarily by a Long-Term Human-Centered or NF perspective, Infrastructure includes the wide range of Social Support Services that are absolutely necessary for communities as a whole not just to function, but to thrive. The focus is strictly on human, not technical, connectedness. It not only includes expanding Child Care for working parents, but added support for Seniors. It also includes support for Education from K-12 through college and beyond. In short, the primary emphasis is on the Collective Mental Health and Well-Being of entire communities, if not Society as a whole.

In this way, NF also focuses on Seeing The Big Picture, but it's not an impersonal, but a highly personal one.

Finally, for those whose personalities is governed primarily by a Short-Term Human-Centered perspective, Infrastructure pertains primarily to one's immediate Family and close circle of friends. That is, how do better roads, etc. improve _my_ individual, personal Quality of Life. Anything else is too abstract and pie-in-the-sky!

It's important to note that each of these is not only defined by what it affirms, but equally by that to what it's opposed. Thus, from its perspective, Short-Term Technical is not only down to Earth and supremely practical, but all of the others are completely impractical, self-centered, totally unrealistic. In turn, the others consider it to be narrow-minded, too preoccupied with itself, and cold-hearted. These are merely samples of the intense arguments that not only define, but divide them.

It should come as no surprise that Conservatives generally favor Short-Term Technical and Short-Term Human-Centered while Liberals generally favor Long-Term Technical and Long-Term Human-Centered. More generally, Conservatives and Liberals have very different interpretations of each of the various perspectives.

The hard truth of the matter is that all of them need to work together for by themselves none of them can address all of the challenges facing us, let alone achieve their individual goals. While historically Infrastructure has been limited to Physical matters exclusively, it's been necessarily broadened by the complexities of a modern world. Indeed, it grows more complex with every passing day. For this reason, Coping with Complexity is one of the overarching themes of the book.

The biggest barrier standing in the way is us. At lower levels of Consciousness, one's preferred Psychological Outlook is the only acceptable one. All others are completely lopsided and wrong, if not dangerous. The extreme Politicization of everything in contemporary life has only made things worse.

One of the best, if not only, ways of getting beyond the stranglehold of the Pure Positions is by getting representatives of each perspective who are willing to come together to work in forming a Synthesis Position that incorporates the concerns of all of the perspectives but is not completely beholden to any of one of them. It requires a Higher Level of Expanded Consciousness before one can break the stranglehold of believing that one's basic stance is the only legitimate one, thereby recognizing that all of them are needed to form a comprehensive picture of how things really are.

The Toulmin Argumentation Framework (TAF)

With regard to the arguments/claims of the first two Chapters, ST and NT are key in providing hard facts and multiple perspectives in counteracting the fears that are the driving forces behind the major arguments/claims. But NF and SF are especially critical is assessing how much of the Truth, let alone which kinds, people can bear to hear, especially that which goes against their most fervent beliefs.

A special framework is especially helpful in this regard. In The Uses of Argument,[2] the eminent Philosopher Stephen Toulmin introduced the following schema for analyzing arguments. It's known as The Toulmin Argumentation Framework or TAF for short. It consists of Claims, Evidence, Warrants, Backings, and Rebuttals.

All arguments terminate in a Claim, the end conclusion of a chain of reasoning. Claims are typically of the form, "Given that the case for X has been established beyond all reasonable doubt, therefore, we need to do Y in order to respond to it." Thus, "Given that Masks and Vaccines have proven highly effective in combatting Covid 19, they need to be Mandated!"

If the Claim is the end conclusion of an argument, then the Evidence is the Evidentiary or Factual Base upon which the argument is built. In short, the Evidence is the complete set of Facts in support of the Claim. Thus, in the case of Covid 19, the Evidence is the thousands of trials that have been successfully conducted in developing the vaccines and establishing their efficacy. It's bolstered further by the fact that the vaccines have been given safely given to millions with remarkably few bad outcomes. It's also been shown that those who have not been vaccinated are some nine times more likely to contract Covid 19 and eleven times more likely to die as a result. All of which is key in supporting the Claim that Masks and Vaccines are absolutely essential in combatting the Virus and thereby in curtailing its spread.

The Warrant is one of the most critical parts of an argument. It's the key component that allows one to go from the Evidence to the Claim. In other words, it's the Bridge between the two. In short, it's the If-Then or Because part of an argument. Thus, If the Evidence is True, Then the Claims follows Because….

In the case of Covid 19, given that the process of developing the vaccines has adhered to long-standing, well-established Scientific procedures, the Warrant ensures that the same standards have been adhered to in this case as well. Thus, we are justified in generalizing from a limited sample of people who've been successfully vaccinated to the necessity of vaccinating the entire population as a whole.

The Backing is the underlying support for the Warrant. No matter how strong they are on their surface, all Warrants are only as strong as that which props them up.

In the case of the Virus, the Backing is the general body of Science and that of Epidemiology in particular. That is, the Warrant is justified because it's backed up the general body of Scientific Knowledge. The reputations of eminent scientists such as Dr. Anthony Fauci are also key parts as well.

---

[2] Stephen Toulmin, The Uses of Argument, Cambridge University Press, New York, 2003.

In effect, the Backing is equivalent to a Guarantor. That is, by following accepted procedures, it guarantees that we will collect the right Evidence, interpret it in the right ways, use the right Warrant correctly, and thus arrive at the right, conclusive Claim.

Finally, the Rebuttal is all of the counterarguments and challenges to every part of the main argument. Thus, the Rebuttal argues why the Claim makes no sense at all, is not fully supported by the Evidence, is illogical, etc.; why the Evidence is flawed, flimsy, and weak; why the Warrant is not sufficient to support the Claim; why the Backing is deficient; and why the Rebuttal is more commanding than any of them.

In effect, Chaps. 1 and 2 are Rebuttals to every one of the chief arguments/claims for not getting vaccinated for Covid 19. In terms of the MBPTI, the Rebuttals are primarily ST/ NT. Again, while absolutely necessary, they unfortunately do not move the vast majority of people, especially those who are staunchly committed to their respective positions.

SF/NF takes a completely different tack. While beholden to ST/NT for uncovering key Evidence, it uses highly personal pleas from persons similar to those opposing the vaccines. In other words, the Rebuttals are highly personal stories delivered by those in whom one has implicit trust. While making fundamental use of ST/NT, SF/NF do not deliver them in impersonal terms.

Sadly, the most effective Rebuttals are from those who are full of deep regret for not having taken the vaccines. It's because either they or a loved one is dying. Whatever the case, they are full of regret and remorse. They wished that they had listened to the likes of Dr. Fauci.

It cannot be said enough. All of the perspectives need to work together if any of them are to be effective. They fail to do so at our peril.

Reflections

In terms of the descriptions of the MBPTI in the chapter, which ones describe you best? Which ones are most different from you? Which ones do you have the most difficulty in understanding and thus in communicating with? Does the discussion change your notions of Infrastructure? Why, why not?

Open Access This chapter is licensed under the terms of the Creative Commons Attribution 4.0 International License (http://creativecommons.org/licenses/by/4.0/), which permits use, sharing, adaptation, distribution and reproduction in any medium or format, as long as you give appropriate credit to the original author(s) and the source, provide a link to the Creative Commons license and indicate if changes were made.

The images or other third party material in this chapter are included in the chapter's Creative Commons license, unless indicated otherwise in a credit line to the material. If material is not included in the chapter's Creative Commons license and your intended use is not permitted by statutory regulation or exceeds the permitted use, you will need to obtain permission directly from the copyright holder.

Chapter 4
Regulating Tech Is Only Half of the Job

> …[the] 'engagement-based ranking'—the system within Facebook more commonly known as 'the algorithm'-that chooses which posts, out of thousands of options, to rank at the top of users' feeds is [in Facebook whistleblower Frances Haugen's words] doomed to amplify the worst in us…[1]

Nonetheless, as important and necessary as it is, regulating Tech is at best only half of the job. The fundamental issue is that we need Technologists who have a deep appreciation and understanding of the Humanities and Social Sciences, and Humanists and Social Scientists who have an equally deep appreciation and understanding of Technology.

Once again, there is no better example of the need than the fact that there were no simulations of all the systems that would be affected by Covid 19. It cannot be emphasized enough that Epidemiologists have been warning for years of the serious possibilities of major Pandemics and have thus done numerous simulations for them. But to my knowledge, no one has proposed let alone performed simulations with regard to how the Economy, Mental Health of Children and the Population as a Whole, Nursing Homes, Schools, Working Conditions, and so forth would not only be seriously affected, but impact each other. For instance, no one contemplated how due to unsafe working conditions and the constant stress of dealing with those suffering from the Virus, Nurses and Pharmaceutical Technicians would quit their jobs in droves.

The point is that Pandemics are not under any obligation to respect the ways in which we've "organized", better yet "disorganized", the world.

If ever an organization needed to be regulated, it's Facebook. Recent articles in both The New York Times and The Wall Street Journal paint a picture of an organization that is a menace in every which way.[2] Stronger still, as unlikely as it is, it needs to be thoroughly dismantled. At the very least, the entire senior leadership

---

[1] Text.

[2] Mike Issac, "A Quandary At Facebook Over Its Tools," The New York Times, Tuesday, October 26, 2021, pp. A1 and A 15.

needs to be replaced. Unfortunately, without changing the underlying culture, even this will not suffice in getting it to behave responsibly.

What makes Facebook so egregious is that it knew for certain that its policies were putting the lives of young girls directly at risk by how it portrayed their looks and bodies and thus encouraged them to be. By relentlessly and unfairly comparing themselves to others, they were subjected to endless amounts of shaming. Saddest of all, it led to reported attempts of suicide.

Once again, it cannot be emphasized enough that it bears major responsibility for aiding and abetting the spread of false information about the vaccines.

But Facebook's egregious behavior goes far beyond its policies alone. Its very operating mechanisms were explicitly designed to hook users. It does it by deliberately feeding endless cycles of messages that play upon their users' insecurities thereby shaming them endlessly. In short, its algorithms were deliberately designed to provoke and thus amplify the most harmful and dangerous attitudes and behaviors.

Even when the dire effects of its policies were brought repeatedly to the attention of senior management by subordinates, Facebook persisted in its irresponsible behavior. No matter how they were obtained, profits trumped everything else.[3]

From being a prime distributor of Dis and Misinformation, allowing Conspiracy Theories to run rampant, providing a vehicle for the direct interference in our elections, Facebook is the epitome of the Socially Irresponsible Organization. It's lacking in any deep sense of Ethical Responsibility.

The "bottom line" is that self-regulation is not only a "joke," but a complete failure.

This only raises the thorny question regarding what can and cannot be regulated. There is no question that harmful behavior and policies can. But at best that's only half of the issue. The remaining components are not only just as critical, but go far beyond regulation per se.

First and foremost is the underlying Ideology upon which Tech rests. It's what I call The Technological Mindset.[4] Fundamental is the core belief that Technology is the solution to all of our problems, including those created by Technology itself. As such, it must be as free and as unencumbered as possible so that it can do its essential job of reinventing the future including the total redesign of our bodies and minds. Technologists need therefore to focus only on the positive benefits of their marvelous inventions. The negatives are the province of others. Talk about critical arguments that need challenging!

All of this is of course bolstered by the Psycho-Social Development of Technologists, or more accurately it's lack thereof. Technology is primarily a "Young Person's game." I say "Young-Person" deliberately. For having been involved with STEM my entire academic career, I've observed the arrested development of far too many Technologists. They are virtually unable and unwilling to

---

[3] Sheera Frankel and Cecilia Kang, An Ugly Truth: Inside Facebook's Battle for Domination, Harper, New York, 2021.

[4] Ian I. Mitroff, Technology Run Amok: Crisis Management in the Digital Age, Palgrave Macmillan, New York, 2019.

think of the Negative, Unintended Consequences of their work, let alone how their marvelous creations will be deliberately abused and misused by nefarious actors for despicable purposes.

Putting together those with similar attitudes into tight-knit groups and organizations only reinforces such immature attitudes and irresponsible behavior. It's directly responsible for the creation of organizations whose Cultures are the epitome of Social Irresponsibility. The result is a continual stream of highly Unethical behavior.

While actions and policies can and should be regulated, the other key components unfortunately cannot. To change the mindset of Technologists requires a massive overhaul of the curricula that are the underlying basis of STEM. By insisting that Ethics be a key component of every course, the hope is that this will help hasten the Psycho-Social development of Technologists. In this regard, the Humanities and Social Sciences are equally critical. They need as well to be key components of every course as well.

Changing the culture of Tech organizations, especially those currently in existence, is another matter. It's estimated that Culture is responsible for up to 80% and more of what goes on in organizations.[5] It dictates what're regarded as acceptable topics for discourse and how to talk about them, how to defer to superiors, how to dress, etc. More often than not, it means going along with behaviors and policies that violate one's deepest convictions. Such is the power of groups and our need to belong.

Because the changes required are so many and so difficult, we can expect Tech companies to keep doing more of the same. But in doing so, they are their own worst enemy. They are the biggest factor prompting their undoing.

Finally, while this chapter has focused primarily on Technology and Tech organizations, the very same issues apply generally to individuals and organizations of all kinds. The groups to which we belong and thereby impact our lives are insistent in reinforcing what they regard as acceptable attitudes and behavior. Especially in today's world, the arguments/claims of the first two chapters are made even more powerful by virtue of their being reinforced constantly via Social Media.

Reflections

How do the arguments and ideas of the chapter strike you? Are they overly critical of Technology? Are they fair, unfair? Why, why not? Can you put your reactions in the form of a Toulmin Argument-Based Structure? How would the different Myers-Briggs Types respond?

---

[5] Ian I. Mitroff and Ralph H. Kilmann, The Psychodynamics of Enlightened Leadership: Coping with Chaos, Springer, New York, 2021.

Open Access This chapter is licensed under the terms of the Creative Commons Attribution 4.0 International License (http://creativecommons.org/licenses/by/4.0/), which permits use, sharing, adaptation, distribution and reproduction in any medium or format, as long as you give appropriate credit to the original author(s) and the source, provide a link to the Creative Commons license and indicate if changes were made.

The images or other third party material in this chapter are included in the chapter's Creative Commons license, unless indicated otherwise in a credit line to the material. If material is not included in the chapter's Creative Commons license and your intended use is not permitted by statutory regulation or exceeds the permitted use, you will need to obtain permission directly from the copyright holder.

Chapter 5
The Socially Responsible Organization: The Critical Cast of Players

In the last chapter, I discussed why Tech companies in particular are especially prone to acting and being Socially Irresponsible. We also discussed the major difficulties in changing their behavior.

In this chapter, I want to approach the matter from the complete opposite end. I want to talk about the nature of the Socially Responsible Organization.

There is no end to the critical qualities that an organization needs to possess before it can be said to be Socially Responsible. But surely one of the most important is its fervent desire to do as much as humanly possible to anticipate and thereby thwart as many of the unanticipated and unintended consequences, and thereby the inherent dangers, of its products and services.

To say that such a task is onerous is putting it mildly. It calls for the broadest possible set of skills and talents imaginable. It demands nothing less than Inter and Transdisciplinary thinking of the highest order. More than the vast majority of organizations realize and thus are able to embody, the following disciplines and professions play a key role in whether they are able to come even close to attaining it. In the best of all worlds, it means having the following cast of players with advanced degrees and experience in major positions. Since this is beyond the capabilities of most organizations, it requires an Advisory Board with as many of the chief players on it as possible:

Clinical Psychologists
Child Development Experts
Organizational Psychologists
Legal Experts
Political Scientists
Crisis Management Experts
Medical Experts
Journalists

Given that the products and services of an organization are capable of being used in ways of causing severe emotional harm to its users, especially the young, elderly, and more vulnerable members of society—Social Media are again the primary culprit—Clinical Psychologists play an indispensable role in anticipating such dire effects. Indeed, what are the critical Warning Signs that one needs to monitor carefully that precede the likely occurrence of harmful events? Hopefully, with appropriate warnings, one can thereby act preemptively thus preventing them from happening. Once again, what does it say about the emotional and Ethical fiber of an organization as in the case of Facebook that it knowingly caused harm in its relentless pursuit of profits "at any cost" [pun intended]?

This is not to say that Clinical Psychologists are prefect by any means in uncovering potential problems, but that properly engaged, they are invaluable in ferreting out the potential ill effects of an organization's products and services. In effect, Chap. 2 made use of Clinical Psychology by means of a deeper analysis of the disturbed reasoning responsible for the arguments/claims for not getting vaccinated.

(To be perfectly candid, while I'm a Fellow of The American Psychological Association for my work in General Psychology, and I'm a lifelong student of Psychoanalytic Thought, I am not a Clinician.)

Similarly, since all Technologies have the potential to affect children, whether they are its primary intended users or not, Experts in Child Development also play an invaluable role. The point is that in today's world, children have access to and are affected by everything around them, especially if it's not intended for them and therefore off-limits.

Organizational Psychologists are equally critical. The Culture of an organization is crucial in explaining why Unethical Behavior is not only accepted, but allowed to flourish.

To emphasize an earlier point, the Culture of organizations is so powerful that it accounts for up to 80% of their behavior. It's so commanding that it forces people to go along with attitudes and behaviors that clearly violate their most sacred and deeply held convictions.

Political Scientists, Sociologists, and Legal Experts are vital in ascertaining whether the products and services favor certain members of the public while systematically disadvantaging others, not to mention portraying them in unfavorable terms. Will they promote division and divisiveness? Will they set family members and longtime friends against one another? Do they promote racism, homophobia, and other forms of prejudice and the maltreatment of others? As in the case of Social Media, do they feed on and amplify our worst instincts and insecurities?

In terms of Crisis Management, will the products and services not only cause enumerable crises for the communities and larger society of which they are a part, but for the members of an organization as well, especially those who are willing to speak out and contest its business practices? I say more about this in the last chapter.

Given that future Pandemics are virtually guaranteed to occur, Medical Experts can help prepare an organization for their disastrous effects on its members and the communities in which they live and serve. Even more, they can help identify the ways in which an organization can contribute to containing versus furthering the Pandemic.

5 The Socially Responsible Organization: The Critical Cast of Players   27

While these only touch on the wide variety of academic disciplines and professions that are vital in ensuring the health, safety, and well-being of the users of an organization's products and services, they are sufficient to show the general nature of what's required if an organization is to have any hope of even recognizing, let alone curtailing, the unanticipated consequences and ill effects of its products and services.

One of the most vital players are Journalists. Indeed, if I had only one key recommendation to make, it would be to hire an Ex Investigative Reporter to conduct intensive interviews with as many members of an organization as possible. The goal is to uncover as many potential crises as possible for which they and their organization will be held responsible, and thus portrayed in the worst possible light and thereby judged harshly. In other words, properly used, Journalists serve as key Early Warning Signals of potential crises. Failing to attend to such Signals is the cause of far too many crises. Facebook is once again guilty as charged.

Indeed, a recent cover of The Week showed a highly unflattering picture of Mark Zuckerberg holding a can of gasoline with the letter "f" emblazoned on it, thereby pouring gas on a fire symbolic of Facebook's "incendiary influence" on the world.[1] For another, in prominent op-eds, The New York Times called explicitly for the resignation of Zuckerberg.[2] It's completely beyond the pale as to how anyone and any organization can survive such horrid portrayals and strident demands for change.

I'm the first to admit how daunting the task described in this chapter is. I'm aware of no organization that even comes close to doing all of the above. Indeed, even if an organization is more than willing, it's generally too much to do all at once. One has no choice but to start slow and build as many coalitions as one can both inside and outside of an organization as possible.

The Chief Legal Officer of an organization is not only the natural starting point, but a key internal Stakeholder. Charged as they are with protecting it legally, they are often the senior most officers that are privy to the full range of potential crises and threats to which their organization is subject. Indeed, as much as possible, it's their basic job to protect the organization from them.

Unfortunately, many organizations and their Chief Officers do not see it this way. And so they stumble from one crisis to another until the organization finally implodes, taking all those who depend on it down with it.

---

[1] The Week, November 5, 2021.
[2] Kara Swisher, "The Zuckerberg Era Is Over," The New York Times, Wednesday, October 27, 2021, p. A23.

Postscript: Meta Mistakes: It's All in a Name

Facebook's rebranding itself as Meta only proves further how completely out of touch it is with even the most minimal understanding of human behavior. If it were more in touch, it would have contemplated a very different set of names. For names are more than just convenient brands. They are major signifiers to the world of the basic soul and spirit of an organization.

In terms of the Myers-Briggs Personality Typology Inventory, the names that the different Types would give to an organization provides further evidence with regard to the nature of the Socially Responsible Organization. The names flow directly from their main concerns.

Short-Term Technical or STs are concerned primarily with the continued profitability and thereby the very existence of an organization. To help ensure their continued survival, they strive to provide as many detailed rules as possible for the safe and reliable use and operation of their products and services. To guarantee that they are indeed used as intended, they collect enumerable statistics with regard to how people actually use them. In this way, they specify more rules as needed as well as undertaking efforts to educate their users. Indeed, as a general consideration, they believe that all problems can be addressed by specifying as many detailed rules as possible. The names that best suits them are Dependable/Reliable Inc., Safe and Steady, or something to the like.

Long-Term Technical or NTs are concerned primarily with identifying serious unmet needs and inventing innovative products and services that satisfy them. The key word is "Innovative." They want nothing more than to be out front of everybody and thereby "stake their claim to being first." The names that best suits them are Innovation Inc., Out Front, or something to the like.

With its emphasis on ever expanding connectivity, Meta certainly falls within the scope. But the thing to note is that it only does it for NT, not for the other Personality Types.

Long-Term Human-Centered or NFs are concerned with products and services that serve the collective good, especially those that bring us together and thus bridge and heal the enormous divides between us. The names that best suits them are Community First, Working Together, All In Together, or something to the like.

Short-Term Human-Centered or SFs are concerned primarily with products and services that help them to achieve their personal goals, especially those which help heal whatever divisions exist within their immediate families and close circle of friends. The names that best suits them are We're Family, Here For You, Trust, or something to the like.

To reiterate, the names we concoct reveal a great deal about us. They are not trivial in the slightest. Ideally, one would choose a name that would appeal to all of the Types. It would be something like Working for You.

Finally, what does one do when the name of one's company matches latest variants of Covid 19? Delta and Omicron are primary cases in point. Talk about the need for Crisis Management!

Reflections

Can you identify an organization that you consider to be Socially Responsible? What do you know about it, especially how it got that way? Was it that way from the very beginning? What does it say about the education and values its founders?

Conversely, what organization(s) would you identify as being Socially Irresponsible? What do you know about them such that they are that way?

Open Access This chapter is licensed under the terms of the Creative Commons Attribution 4.0 International License (http://creativecommons.org/licenses/by/4.0/), which permits use, sharing, adaptation, distribution and reproduction in any medium or format, as long as you give appropriate credit to the original author(s) and the source, provide a link to the Creative Commons license and indicate if changes were made.

The images or other third party material in this chapter are included in the chapter's Creative Commons license, unless indicated otherwise in a credit line to the material. If material is not included in the chapter's Creative Commons license and your intended use is not permitted by statutory regulation or exceeds the permitted use, you will need to obtain permission directly from the copyright holder.

Chapter 6
Dis Versus Mis-Information: Unexpected Insights from Covid19

Once again, the chapter calls attention to the distressing fact that one of the least anticipated, and thus least prepared for, aspects of the Pandemic was the spate of arguments that poured forth in favor of not getting vaccinated for the Virus. This is in spite of the fact that similar types of arguments were parts of previous Pandemics. It's thereby one of the most serious ways in which we failed to learn from earlier crises.

If ever we needed to learn the critical lessons that Covid 19 has to teach so that we can be better prepared for future Pandemics, surely that time is now.

One of the key points of Chaps. 1 and 2 is that one of the least anticipated consequences of Covid19, and therefore least planned for, was the spate of bizarre and outlandish arguments/claims that were constantly bandied about by those who are bitterly opposed to taking the vaccines. They are so far beyond the pale of ordinary thought such that they are literally unthinkable, at least to those possessing the most minimum amount of reasonableness.

Yes, once again, it's unfortunately the case that such arguments are not entirely without precedent for they've accompanied all important Public Health outbreaks such as HIV and SARS. Denial is regrettably a major accompaniment of all events that are too painful to comprehend, let alone bear. Still, why weren't they better anticipated by the Medical Community and Social Scientists working together? Once again, if they had, would it have helped lower the resistance to the taking of the vaccines, thereby upping the rates of vaccinations, and thus hopefully stemming the spread of a deadly disease?

But then it would have required the intense cooperation of diverse disciplines working together. Indeed, before then, it requires mutual respect and understanding.

What's supremely sad, if not tragic, is that the vaccines that were produced in record times were for the express purpose of protecting as many people as possible from a fatal disease, thus curtailing its spread.

Recall that the arguments/claims for not getting vaccinated fell into distinct clusters thus bolstering one another. First and foremost is the Hoax Cluster, namely that

Virus is not real, and thus not deserving of any attention. It was aided by its natural ally, the Conspiracy/Paranoia Cluster, which asserts without any proof whatsoever that by surreptitiously placing micro-chips in the vaccines, the Virus has been deliberately fomented by the Government to spy on us. Not only can the Government thereby track our every whereabouts, and most of all our thoughts, but it can then control us and take away our precious freedoms and liberties. Another important group is the Invulnerability Cluster, namely that "If in the highly unlikely case that the Virus is real, I'm immune to it." The Product Defect Cluster is the absurd and unfounded claim that the Vaccine, not the Virus, is the true danger since it's responsible for causing the Virus in the first place. It thus completely reverses the correct order of causality. Worst of all, the Virus was deliberately placed in the vaccines by the Government in order to infect as many people as possible. While these do not exhaust all of so-called arguments/claims, they more than capture the general spirit of the madness.

The clusters apply to virtually all of the important issues with which we are struggling. Climate Change comes immediately to mind. The Hoax Cluster takes the form of outright Climate Denial. To those who believe it's a Hoax, it's a perfect example of more unwanted Government Intrusion into our lives. Thus, Paranoia is a prominent feature as well. Invulnerability takes the form that its effects are exaggerated and thereby completely overblown.

Consider how they apply to Dis and Misinformation. Whereas Misinformation is supposedly unintentional, Disinformation is intentional in that it's deliberately concocted. Be this as it may, the general clusters apply equally to both. Indeed, more often than not, it's supremely difficult to distinguish between the two.

Consider the general outcomes of Dis and Misinformation. Both play major roles in the instigation and spread of Anger and Distrust, Disengagement from Public and Private Life, Greater Divisiveness and Polarization, and especially the Promotion of Widespread Fear and Panic.

The Hoax Cluster works both ways. The first is claiming that there is a Hoax when there is not. It's thereby one of the major forms of Dis and Misinformation. The second is claiming that there is not a Hoax when there definitively is. It cannot be stressed enough that both forms apply equally to Dis and Misinformation. To reiterate, either is capable of Causing Havoc and thus of promoting Widespread Anger, Fear, and Distrust.

The most prominent example is the Big Lie, namely that Donald Trump won the last election when there is abundant proof that he did not. Just as bad are efforts by Republican lawmakers to whitewash the January 6, 2021 attacks on the U.S Capitol by among other things arguing that "it's time to focus on the future, not dwell on the past," thereby blocking an honest examination of one of the worst challenges to American Democracy.

More generally, the Hoax Cluster is not only capable of Raising False Hopes, but of Dashing Honest Ones; Creating Versus Ignoring Legitimate Crises and Threats; Creating Unrealistic Expectations Versus Suppressing Realistic Ones; Setting Parties Against One Another and in this regard Creating False Allies and Enemies, etc.

The Invulnerability Cluster applies equally as well. In this case, the claim is that one is Invulnerable when one is not. The exact opposite is the false claim that one is Vulnerable when one is in fact secure and well-protected from whatever threats are imagined. One of the most unfortunate examples is the unfounded claims of parents that by virtue of their young ages, their children are naturally immune to the Virus when they are not. As before, children must be generally protected from anything that poses a threat to their esteem, self-image, and self-worth. In short, they must be protected from anything disturbing.

To reiterate, the Defect Cluster wrongly attributes Cause and Effects. Thus, not only does it confuse them, but it attributes the wrong things to each. In effect, it leads one down the wrong paths. It's directly responsible for what are known as Type 3 Errors, Solving the Wrong Problems Precisely, thus diverting attention away from the most important problems.

Once again, the worst consequences are Rampant Fear, Unconstrained Panic, and Paranoia.

One of the most serious cases is the fallacious claim that Mandates for vaccinations are entirely new and that President Biden is thereby clearly to blame for instituting them. Nothing could be further from the truth. Mandates for serious diseases go back as far as George Washington who ordered them for smallpox.

If only Dis and Misinformation were so easily dispelled by supplying Accurate and True Information. If only it were that simple. Unfortunately, such is not the case, especially in a world where they're constantly manufactured and distributed by the latest technologies such as so-called Social Media, more accurately labelled Anti-Social Media.

To emphasize an earlier point, as best we know, the most effective way of countering fallacious beliefs is by means of close personal friends who've not only been down the same false paths, but have the courage to admit that they were wrong. It's as close to a truly heroic act that most of us ever get.

Arguments big and small, true and false, literally make the world go round. They are the foundations upon which our lives are built. Challenging false arguments/claims has never been more important, and yet more arduous.

Postscript: A Needed Success Story

One of the most successful efforts in combatting Dis and Misinformation is that of New York City.[1] Its success is due to identifying new types of Disinformation and their sources and then putting out facts as soon as possible to counteract them. For instance, it was wrongly claimed that the vaccines increased infertility, were designed to "annihilate Christianity and the Polish Nation." In other words, once

---

[1] Mara Gay, "Not Everyone in N.Y. Wanted the Coronavirus to Lose," The New York Times, Wednesday, November 3, 2021, p. A23.

again, they fed on deep insecurities. The campaign to dispel them was so successful that it increased vaccination rates among Black residents by 15%.

The chief lesson is that even if facts don't necessarily persuade everyone, they are essential nonetheless in reaching critical segments of the population.

As an important footnote, young people have taken the lead in getting the correct facts out to one another thus once again showing the power of personal touch.

Reflections

Think of as many examples as you can where you or your family have been exposed to information that later proved to be false. What were the sources of the Dis or Misinformation? Why did they seem credible? What was key in convincing you that they were false?

Open Access This chapter is licensed under the terms of the Creative Commons Attribution 4.0 International License (http://creativecommons.org/licenses/by/4.0/), which permits use, sharing, adaptation, distribution and reproduction in any medium or format, as long as you give appropriate credit to the original author(s) and the source, provide a link to the Creative Commons license and indicate if changes were made.

The images or other third party material in this chapter are included in the chapter's Creative Commons license, unless indicated otherwise in a credit line to the material. If material is not included in the chapter's Creative Commons license and your intended use is not permitted by statutory regulation or exceeds the permitted use, you will need to obtain permission directly from the copyright holder.

Chapter 7
Compromise Is Key to Our Learning to Live Together: The Resolution of Key Issues Is Not Possible Without It

In a previously published blog,[1] I asked whether Moderates and Progressives can learn to "work together." Given the enormous differences between them, the broader question is whether they can co-exist and thus learn to "live together." While Progressives played a key role in President Biden's victory and early successes, it's putting it mildly to say that things have turned South in recent days. Overall, his job approval ratings are at an abysmal low.

Take Climate Change. While both Moderates and Progressives agree that it's a major problem that needs immediate attention, Progressives insist that it has to be at the center of any deal, or there's no deal at all. It's no exaggeration to say that they're in a prolonged state of serious Conflict. The key question is what if anything can be done to resolve it.

My life-long colleague and good friend Ralph H. Kilmann and his colleague Ken Thomas have developed the most comprehensive approach to the management of Conflict of which I know. It shows in no uncertain terms the Psychological processes that need to be acknowledged and worked through if one is not just to be able to work together productively, but more importantly, to live together harmoniously. It thus adds a further dimension to our deeper understanding of human behavior.

Two dimensions are key to the Kilmann-Thomas framework. They are best understood in terms of a pie. The first deals with how much of a pie a person wants solely for him, herself, or they. The second deals with how much of a pie one is willing to give to another. The first dimension is best captured by the catchphrase "Get," and the second as "Give."

Whatever the issue, if one always strives to "get a whole pie solely for oneself," then one's Conflict Handling Style is Competing. If on the other hand, "one habitually gives a pie to another," then one is Accommodating. If both parties strive to avoid a Conflict situation altogether, and hence neither one of them gets any of the

---

[1] https://www.nationofchange.org/2021/09/28/can-moderates-and-progressives-find-any-way-to-work-together/

pie, then they are Avoiders. If both parties are satisfied with half of the pie, then they are Compromisers. Finally, if both parties are willing to work together as Collaborators, then then in principle they can expand the pie such that they both get a full one.

Notice how each of these play a key role in making important decisions. If one party is clearly an expert in a critical area, then Accommodating to her, him, or they is not only appropriate, but best. By the same token, the party who is an expert in a particular area is justified in asserting their position, and thus in being Competitive. If in comparison to other issues the particular one is not important, then Avoiding is called for. Compromise is appropriate if that's the best one can get, and further, if it preserves "group cohesiveness." And while it often takes the most time and energy to achieve, Collaborating is best of all because it results in a "win-win" for all parties.

Once again, Covid 19 is the premiere case in point. It requires that one defer and thus Accommodate to the expertise of those more knowledgeable and qualified than one is, especially when it comes to Medical matters.

Notice that not only are these descriptions of their key attributes but of the main arguments upon which each of their positions rest. So once again, it boils down to arguments.

Ideally, one would have the ability to enact for all five conflict modes: Competing, Accommodating, Avoiding, Compromising, and Collaborating. Depending on the particular situation, one would then be able to respond appropriately.

If this were the case, then the four Myers-Briggs Personality Types would be able to work together harmoniously. Indeed, it's an essential requirement for their being able to do so.

Importantly, notice how they are affected by the states of mind that we described in Chap. 2. Take Paranoia. In this case, one distrusts all others so that the Conflict Modes collapse into Fight, Flight, or Freeze. Fight if one feels that there is no alternative but to assert one's position. Parenthetically, it does not necessarily mean to Fight physically, but to assert oneself aggressively. Flight if one feels threatened and has to leave a situation at all costs. Freeze if one feels paralyzed and literally unable to move.

In the end, the prime issue is what's more important, winning or preserving group harmony? Compromising is as much about living together amicably than it's about resolving key issues. Indeed, one is not possible without the other.

Just when we need it more than ever, Compromise is more elusive than at any time.

Reflections

As before, what Conflict Styles best describe you? Which ones are least like you? What are the obstacles to your getting along with those Styles that are least like you? Does the chapter help in this regard?

Open Access This chapter is licensed under the terms of the Creative Commons Attribution 4.0 International License (http://creativecommons.org/licenses/by/4.0/), which permits use, sharing, adaptation, distribution and reproduction in any medium or format, as long as you give appropriate credit to the original author(s) and the source, provide a link to the Creative Commons license and indicate if changes were made.

The images or other third party material in this chapter are included in the chapter's Creative Commons license, unless indicated otherwise in a credit line to the material. If material is not included in the chapter's Creative Commons license and your intended use is not permitted by statutory regulation or exceeds the permitted use, you will need to obtain permission directly from the copyright holder.

Chapter 8
Coping with a Complex Messy World: Education for the Twenty-First Century and Beyond

In the end, this book is not only about the enumerable arguments that we are required to make in order to function, but equally about a world that challenges us in every which way. The short of it is that we live in a world whose complexity grows by the nanosecond. Unfortunately, few have been taught the full complement of skills necessary to make sense of and thereby cope with a complex, messy world. And yet, our very survival hinges on it.

As I've argued throughout, it requires our ability to reason critically and thus to give the most serious arguments/claims the intense scrutiny they demand. Anything less is irresponsible. In this regard, as much as CRT has rightly stood for Critical Race Theory, it needs just as much to stand for Critical Reasoning Theory.

Because they're all highly interdependent, we could start with any one of the critical skills that are necessary in today's world and beyond. But since the kind of knowledge needed to deal with a complex, messy world is paramount, Philosophy is a natural starting point. Further, if any Philosophic system is especially suited for dealing with complexity, it's the Philosophical School of Pragmatism. Its essence is best captured in terms of a brief definition of what it regards as the Truth, especially how to achieve it. While the definition is significant in and of itself, its importance is made even greater by the unparalleled insights it offers into the nature of complexity.

In brief, Pragmatism is best summarized by the following: "Truth is that which Makes a Profound Ethical and Spiritual Difference in the Quality of Our Lives." Thus, unlike other Philosophic systems for producing knowledge, according to Pragmatism, Epistemology, Ethics, Spirituality, and Aesthetics are not only interrelated, but inseparable. In short, Truth does not consist of abstract facts, propositions, and theories alone. In a word, Truth requires ST, NT, NF, and SF working together. To be sure, it definitively does not consist of ST or NT alone.

The true importance of the definition is that it's the Philosophical Basis of The Socially Responsible Organization.

To elaborate, Epistemology is the systematic means by which produce and thereby secure Formal Knowledge. Ethics is the means by which we know what is

Right Ethically and what we need to do in order to bring it about. Spirituality is the feelings deep inside of us by which we know that there is more to the Human Condition than our bodies and Pure Thought alone. The phrase Quality of Life is a stand-in for Aesthetics, that is, what's Harmonious and thereby makes life Pleasing for ourselves and others. Finally, the little word "Makes" means that Truth does not consist of a set of Hard Facts, published articles, and books, but a carefully crafted set of Ethical Actions designed to Right a set of Wrongs. In other words, Ethical Actions are not only the primary means by which Truth is secured, but its very essence. To reiterate, Truth neither consists of nor is produced ST and NT alone.

The true significance of Pragmatism is that it leads to a deeper understanding of complex, messy systems, and thus of the complexity with which we are faced.

The late, great distinguished Social System's Educator and Scientist par excellence, Russell L. Ackoff appropriated the word "Mess" to stand for a whole system of problems that were so highly bound—thus interrelated—and constantly changing in direct response to one another such that one couldn't take any of the so-called individual problems out of the Mess and attempt to analyze them on their own without doing irreparable damage both to the fundamental nature of the so-called individual problems and the entire Mess of which they were an integral part. In other words, looking at problems in isolation violated one of the key properties of a Mess, namely all of the critical interactions between them. Indeed, interactions are the key attributes of every Mess. In this way, the notion of "self-standing individual problems" is a complete misrepresentation of today's world. As such, it needs to be thoroughly abandoned and thus put to rest.

(As an important aside, Ackoff was the first PhD student at Penn of my Philosophical mentor, C. West Churchman, with whom I studied at UC Berkeley. In turn, Churchman was a student of E.A. Singer who was one of William James' best students. And of course, James was one of the principal founders of Pragmatism. Thus, if intellectually speaking, Singer is my Grandfather, then James is my Great Grandfather, a matter of which I couldn't be prouder. My link with Pragmatism is especially strong indeed.)

There's another important consideration that makes things both much more interesting and complex. The late, distinguished UC Berkeley Architectural planner Horst Rittel introduced the notion of Wicked Problems. Wicked Problems are the complete opposite of Tame Problems, of which Exercises are the prime examples. The enormous attention given to Exercises throughout Education is due to the fact that they're Bounded and Well-Structured, thus lowering the enormous anxieties and stress that are often associated with problem solving, if not Schooling in general.

"$X+5=11$, find X" is a typical example. Thus, following the classic rules of Algebra, everyone is expected to get the single right answer, $X=6$. Furthermore, once solved, Tame Problems stay solved forever. Not so with Wicked Problems. No single academic discipline or profession has the final say in either their definition or solution. Furthermore, they are constantly changing so that a solution for one time is not necessarily one for others.

Putting the two together, the result is Wicked Messes. All of the key problems with which we are faced—Climate Change, the Economy, Extreme Divisiveness and Polarization, Homelessness, Women's Rights, etc.—are Wicked Messes. But things are even more complicated. Because at least one problem of every Mess is part of every other Mess, all Wicked Messes are thereby part of the larger Wicked Mess best described as The Societal or World Mess. In short, all of the known problems of Society and the World are deeply interconnected.

In this way, Pragmatism not only forces us to grapple with, but challenges us constantly to surmount the immense turmoil associated with the most complex entities imaginable. Psychology is thereby a key element with regard to our ability to bear with and thus cope with complexity. In short, one's state of mind is a key component of every Wicked Mess. Not only does one need to able to tolerate high degrees of uncertainty, but to appreciate the widest possible diversity of Expert Opinion. (Once again, notice the direct bearing on Covid 19.) Indeed, one needs to seek it out. Once again, without it, one is doomed to falling prey to the Errors of the Third Kind: "Solving the Wrong Problems Precisely." Before one makes the critical decision as to which problem one needs to solve, multiple perspectives are absolutely essential. In this way, NT and NF play critical roles in revealing alternatives.

Since crises are an ever-present feature of today's world, Crisis Management (CM) is also an integral component of coping with Wicked Messes. Indeed, every Wicked Mess both contains and leads to enumerable crises.

(The Epilogue contains a sampling of the various kinds of crises that are connected with and thus are integral parts of Covid 19.)

CM fundamentally consists of Thinking the Unthinkable and then doing everything in one's power to prevent it from happening. But since crises both happen to and are often the result of the faulty and irresponsible—read "Unethical"—behavior of organizations, specialized knowledge of organizations is also a critical ingredient in coping with complexity. This is not to say that all crises are thereby the direct fault of every organization. However, not considering their possibility and thus not preparing for them is.

In order to be as prepared as possible, CM not only necessitates understanding what organizations need to do Before, During, and After crises, but especially why far too many are resistant to CM.

The set of activities that encompass Before are first of all the consideration of as many Worst-Case Scenarios as possible. Namely, how crises can and will occur in the most unimaginable ways—again see the Epilogue—and at the most inopportune times. Second, that none of the known types of crises should be discounted. Rather, the key question is, "What is the form that say Product Tampering or Domestic Terrorism can and will assume such that it's either our fault or does insurmountable damage to us?" Third, how do we identify and overcome the barriers that stand in the way of making CM a key priority for our organization? Fourth, how do we form and maintain Crisis Management Teams (CMTs) throughout our entire organization that will meet regularly, assess our susceptibility to crises, and address if our preparations are adequate?

During involves enacting all of one's Before preparations. If one is not prepared Before, then a crisis will only make things worse for a crisis is the worst time to develop the skills necessary to deal with it. And After involves the most brutal, no-holds-bared assessment of what one did right versus wrong so that one is better prepared for future crises. In other words, Learning the Lessons from Past Crises is key. Sadly, as I've pointed out throughout, we failed to learn key lessons from previous Pandemics.

One of the most critical of all activities is coming to terms with the different forms and sources of Denial.

In Chaps. 1 and 2 we examined a series of arguments/claims that have been constantly bandied about for *not* getting vaccinated for Covid 19. As bad as the individual arguments/claims were, they were made even worse by the highly disturbing fact that they reinforced one another by forming into tight clusters thereby bolstering one another even more.

While they are by far one of the most destressing outcomes of Covid 19, the situation is made worse by the fact they are a direct reflection of the sad state of Reason in general. The greatest downfall is that they impede our collective ability to tackle the important issues facing us. In short, they are Denial writ large.

The point is that all of the Clusters are part of every Wicked Mess. Whatever the particular case, there are always voices claiming that it's a Hoax, and so on. For this reason alone, Critical Thinking—surfacing and rebutting fallacious arguments/claims—is one of the most important skills in dealing with Wicked Messes.

Coping with Wicked Messes calls for all the fortitude and skills we can muster. Nothing less will suffice.

In the end, either we are prepared for the most godawful arguments that accompany every major crisis, or we will continue to suffer their most horrific consequences. In this regard, let me close with a recap of the general categories into which the major arguments/claims for not getting vaccinated for Covid 19 fall. They need to be taken with the utmost seriousness for with little modification they apply to virtually all crises.

They are presented in the form of questions for they are nothing less than Existential Questions of the first order:

First, is the Threat Real/Believable/Credible?
Is it Serious Enough to be given Attention?
Am I Safe/Protected?
Whom can I Trust/Believe to Give me Accurate and True Information?
Am I being Mislead by False Information? By the Government? The News Media? Social Media?
Is the Government out to get me?
Are the Vaccines Safe or are they the Cause of the disease? Have they been tested enough?
Am I Dependent on Others or do I Know Best when it comes to my body?
How much Faith am I to put in Authorities? In Science?
How much Certainty do I require before I can Function?

The responses to the above lie on a sharp continuum. They range from extreme cautiousness and concern on the one hand, thus taking Threats seriously, to that of Denial and Dismissal on the other. Since the two sides are always contending, they are thereby an integral part of every crisis, indeed of every Wicked Mess.

It cannot be said enough: Be prepared or suffer the consequences.

Open Access This chapter is licensed under the terms of the Creative Commons Attribution 4.0 International License (http://creativecommons.org/licenses/by/4.0/), which permits use, sharing, adaptation, distribution and reproduction in any medium or format, as long as you give appropriate credit to the original author(s) and the source, provide a link to the Creative Commons license and indicate if changes were made.

The images or other third party material in this chapter are included in the chapter's Creative Commons license, unless indicated otherwise in a credit line to the material. If material is not included in the chapter's Creative Commons license and your intended use is not permitted by statutory regulation or exceeds the permitted use, you will need to obtain permission directly from the copyright holder.

Epilogue

Below is the list of crises with which the modern field of Crisis Management (CM) began. Product Recalls and Product Tampering are listed first because the 1982 poisonings of Tylenol capsules which lead to deaths of seven people in a suburb outside of Chicago is generally credited as the single event most responsible for the creation of CM. Noticeably absent are Public Health crises such as Pandemics which should have been included from the very beginning. Technical crises should have been included as well.

Product Recalls
Product/Service/Logo Tampering
Employee Sabotage
Fires, Explosions, Chemical Spills
Environmental Disasters
Significant Drop in Revenues/Financial
Natural Hazards
Loss of Confidential/Sensitive Information
Terrorism
Ethical Breaches
Government/Regulatory

To emphasize a key point, time and time again we've had to learn that none of the various Types of crises can be taken literally and thereby as applying only to certain kinds of organizations and not to all of them. Every Type is capable of assuming a wide variety of forms such that they are applicable to all organization and industries. Therefore, none of them can be discounted. To do so is to invite disaster.

As a result, if one is to get out in front and do everything one can to prepare for, and hopefully prevent, the worst from happening, CM demands the most creative and expansive thinking possible, thus NT and NF. The plain fact of the matter is that no crisis ever happens exactly as we've imagined it. Thus, constantly Thinking the Unthinkable, and even more preparing for it, is essential.

© The Author(s) 2022
I. I. Mitroff, *The Socially Responsible Organization*, SpringerBriefs in Business, https://doi.org/10.1007/978-3-030-99808-0

If this weren't enough, then the following only adds to the challenge. While crises typically start in one category or Type, they quickly spread and thereby involve all of the others. In short, no crisis is ever—repeat, EVER!—a single crisis. The need to think and act Systemically—read "expansively"—is an absolute requirement if one is to stand any chance of coping with the most diverse array of crises.

Thus, consider the different forms that the Types have assumed with regard to Covid 19.

Product Recalls has to do with the false claims that the vaccines are not safe because they've not been tested adequately. Therefore, they should be withdrawn immediately. To reiterate an earlier fallacious argument/claim, the vaccines, not the Virus, are the problem.

Once again, Product Tampering has to do with the false claims that the Government deliberately planted microchips in the vaccines in order to spy on us. The Government is thereby the enemy.

With regard to Employee Sabotage, the Government is the saboteur!

Fires, Explosions, Chemical Spills refers to the false contention that the vaccines are Toxic, thus furthering the false claim that they're responsible for causing the Virus.

While the Virus is not responsible for causing Environmental Disasters per se it's not a stretch to consider it as one of the worst calamities we've ever faced. In this sense, it's an Environmental Disaster of the first order.

Given that the Pandemic seriously impacted the Economy, the link with Financial Crises is clear.

Natural Hazards reflects the fact that all so-called Natural Disasters bear the direct imprint of Humans, and in this sense, are Human-Caused. After all, it's us not Mother Nature who make the critical decisions where to build houses and to what standards. This is not to minimize in the slightest the terrible suffering that the people of Kentucky have endured recently as a result of the unprecedented destructive tornados to which they've been subject. It is to emphasize that by occurring at the same time as the Pandemic, Natural Hazards exacerbate the worst of both.

The Loss of Sensitive Information is a direct reference to the vast amounts of Dis and Misinformation that have been produced in response to the Pandemic.

Terrorism is without a doubt one of the most serious of all the Types. The refusal by far too many to take the vaccines can be seen as nothing less than explicit acts of Domestic Terrorism. It also represents an Ethical Breach of the highest order. And of course, there have been numerous charges of International Terrorism directed towards foreign powers for failing to inform the world of the Virus in a timely and responsible fashion.

But of them all, explicit death threats directed towards those Public Health officials who've dared Mandated the wearing of masks is the clearest example of Domestic Terrorism.

Finally, the role that Social Media played in both the hyping and distribution of false information with regard to the Virus and vaccines has once again fueled demands for the greater regulation of Tech companies.

These are of course only a few of the many possible interpretations of the different types of crises that apply to Covid 19. I leave it to readers to think of as many more as they can.

Most important of all, my fervent hope is that the above serve as spurs to our collective imagination so that we are better prepared for future Pandemics. Namely, how could we simulate the various ways in which they can occur and even more impact one another? What are the Early Warning Signals that we ought to be monitoring that would give us advance warning of their likely occurrence? How ought Crisis Management Teams to be formed and trained?

These are only a sampling of the many issues involved.

Reflections

For you and you alone, what are the greatest takeaway messages of the book? What can you do better to meet the challenges facing you? What more do you need to understand better?

Index

A
Accommodating, 36
Advisory Board, 25
Algorithm, 21, 22
Anti-Social Media, 33
Arguments, 1, 2, 5, 6, 9, 10, 12, 13, 15–19
Avoiding, 36

B
Backings, 18, 19
Biden, 33, 35
Big Picture, 17
Broadband, 16

C
Characteristics, 3
Chief Legal Officer, 27
Child Care, 17
Child Development Experts, 25, 26
Civics Education, 3
Claims, 2, 5, 6, 9, 10, 12, 15, 18, 19
Climate Change, 16, 32, 35, 40
Clinical Psychologists, 25, 26
Clinical Psychology, 26
Closed System, 3
Collaborating, 36
Collaborators, 36
Collective Mental Health, 9
Collective Mental Health and Well-Being, 17
Collective Mental Illness, 12
Compartmentalization, 12
Competing, 36
Compromise, 36
Compromising, 36
Conflict, 35
Conflict modes, 36
Conflict Styles, 36
Consciousness, 17
Conservative rally, 2
Conservatives and Liberals, 17
Conspiracy, 12
Conspiracy/Paranoia Cluster, 5, 12
Conspiracy Theories, 22
Coping, 42
Correct sequence, 4
Counterarguments, 1, 6
Covid 19, 31, 36, 42
Crises, 27
Crisis Management (CM), 25, 26, 28, 41
Crisis Management Teams (CMTs), 41
Critical Race Theory, 6
Critical Reasoning Theory, 39
Critical skills, 39
Critical Thinking and Civic Responsibility, 5
Culture, 22, 23
Culture of organizations, 26
Cyber-Security, 16

D
Delta, 28
Demented Thinking, 9
Denial, 31
Dependable/Reliable Inc., 28

Designer humans, 5
Dis and Misinformation, 22
Disinformation, 32, 33
Distrust, 11

E
Economy, 40
Epidemiologists, 5, 21
Epistemology, 39
Epitome of the Socially Irresponsible Organization, 22, 23
Ethical Responsibility, 22
Evidence, 18, 19
Ex Investigative Reporter, 27
Extreme cautiousness, 43
Extreme Divisiveness and Polarization, 40–41

F
Facebook, 21, 22, 26–28
Fallacious beliefs, 33
False belief, 1, 4, 5, 11, 12
Fears, 9, 12, 13
Freedom, 1–3, 5, 10, 12

G
Gene-editing technology, 4
Grandiosity, 10–12

H
Healthy Leadership, 9
Higher Level of Expanded Consciousness, 17
HIV, 6
Hoax cluster, 1, 4, 5, 12
Homelessness, 41
Humanities, 21, 23

I
Infrastructure, 15–17
Infrastructure Bill, 15
Innovation Inc., 28
Inter and Transdisciplinary thinking, 25
Intuitive-Feeling or NF, 16
Intuitive-Thinking or NT, 16
Invulnerability Cluster, 1, 5, 6, 12, 33

J
Journalists, 25, 27

L
Legal Experts, 25, 26
Logic and Reason, 9
Logic and thinking, 9
Long-Term Human-Centered, 16, 17, 28
Long-Term People-Oriented, 15
Long-Term Technical, 15–17, 28

M
Masks, 2–4, 10, 11, 18
Medical Experts, 25, 26
Mental Disorders, 5
Meta, 28
Misinformation, 32–34
Myers-Briggs Personality Types, 36
Myers-Briggs Personality Typology (MBPTI), 16, 19
Myers-Briggs Personality Typology Inventory, 28

N
Narcissism, 10–12
Natural Immunity, 9
Nefarious Liberals, 4

O
Obsessive need for Certainty, 12
Omicron, 28
Omnipotent Thinking, 10, 12
Open System, 3
Organizational Psychologists, 25, 26
Out Front, 28

P
Pandemics, 26
Paranoia, 6, 11, 12
Person's special circumstances, 3
Philosophical School of Pragmatism, 39
Physical Structures, 16
Players, 25, 27
Political Divide, 15
Political Scientists, 25, 26
Pragmatism, 39–41
Product Defect Cluster, 5, 12, 32
Progressives, 35
Psychological analysis, 9
Psychological Outlook, 17
Psychological processes, 35
Psycho-Social Development of Technologists, 22

Index

Psychotherapists, 9, 12
Psychotherapy, 9
Public Health, 3
Pure Positions, 17

R
Rebuttals, 18, 19
Right-to-Lifers, 3

S
Safe and Steady, 28
SARS, 6
Self-correcting, 4
Self-image, 33
Self-regulation, 22
Self-worth, 33
Sensing-Feeling (SF), 16
Sensing-Thinking (ST) for short, 16
Serious Mental Distress, 12
Short-Term Human-Centered, 16, 17, 28
Short-Term People-Oriented, 15
Short-Term Technical (STs), 15–17, 28
Socially Irresponsible, 25
Social Media, 26, 33
Social Support Services, 17
Sociologists, 26
Spirituality, 40
Stakeholder, 27

STEM, 22, 23
Synthesis Position, 17

T
Tech organizations, 23
Technological Mindset, 22
Technologists, 21–23
Technology, 21–23
The New York Times, 2, 21, 27
The Uses of Argument, 18
The Wall Street Journal, 21
Thought Disorders, 12
Thwart unintended consequences, 25
Toulmin Argumentation Framework (TAF), 18
Trump, Donald, 32
Truth, 40

U
Unethical behavior, 23, 26

V
Vaccinations, 31
Vaccines, 18
Vulnerability, 6

W
Warrants, 18, 19
Wicked Problems, 40
Widespread Mental Disturbance, 9
Women's Rights, 41

The manufacturer's authorised representative in the EU is Springer Nature Customer Service Centre GmbH, Europaplatz 3, 69115 Heidelberg, Germany. If you have any concerns regarding our products, please contact ProductSafety@springernature.com

Printed and bound by CPI Group (UK) Ltd, Croydon, CR0 4YY

25/03/2026

02078172-0014